HALF WILD

HALF WILD
poems

Mary Rose O'Reilley

Louisiana State University Press
Baton Rouge

Published by Louisiana State University Press
Copyright © 2006 by Mary Rose O'Reilley
Manufactured in the United States of America
An LSU Press Paperback Original
FIRST PRINTING

Designer: Melanie O'Quinn Samaha
Typefaces: Minion, Gotham
Printer and binder: Data Reproductions, Inc.

Library of Congress Cataloging-in-Publication Data

O'Reilley, Mary Rose.
    Half wild : poems / Mary Rose O'reilley.
        p. cm.
    ISBN 0-8071-3162-8 (pbk. : alk. paper)
    I. Title.
PS3615.R456H35   2006
811'.6—dc22

                                                    2005026794

Grateful acknowledgment is made to the editors of *Seeding the Snow,* in which the following poems first appeared: "We Keep Asking the Prairie" (Fall/Winter 2002); "Snowblind" (Fall/Winter 2000); "Boreal Owl" (Spring/Summer 2000). "The Deer's Prayer," "Scholar's Garden," and "Call It a Match " first appeared in "What Sound Does the Soul Make?" by Mary Rose O'Reilley in *Living the Questions: Essays Inspired by the Work of Parker J. Palmer* (San Francisco: Jossey-Bass, an imprint of John Wiley & Sons, 2005), edited by Sam M. Intrator, 52–56.

The author wishes to acknowledge the assistance and support of the Bush Foundation, the Loft Literary Center, the McKnight Foundation, the Sitka Center for Arts and Ecology, and the University of St. Thomas during the writing of this book. She is grateful also to her Loft Mentors, Barney Bush, Sandra Cisneros, and Galway Kinnell; and to her first readers, Peter Crysdale, Deborah Keenan, and Julian O'Reilley. To Mary Oliver, for the blessing of her own work, thank you.

For Jude and Julian O'Reilley

Contents

HALF WILD

Twin

The incubator
was not lens enough
to show me where you flew,
out of the doctor's fingers,

out of the air's restraint.
And all their mirrors
could not lure your breath.
You were the part of me

that gave itself to death.
Sometimes I dream of eyes,
sealed with a membrane
of unknowing

like a mystic's veil,
that open to my glance
without surprise.
Sometimes I dream

of perfect understanding.
Sometimes I snatch
at hands that seem to seek
as through a caul.

Sometimes I waken
With an infant's shriek.

Scene of the Crime Photos

I know
the trajectory
of this crumpled doll
to the bathroom floor.

I know
why the suicide
dropped his glasses.

I know
where you lie
with a rinse of darkness
under your head

in a ruin of faces
tried on,
discarded

in the uncontrollable gush
of words
you should never
have said.

The Girl They Caught

Sometime after midnight
they cut the 12-horse Evinrude,
their boat bumps at the dock.

Your kitchen lamp
defines a cribbage game.
Everything dark is holding.

I hear them come in
without knocking.
They carry the girl in a quilt.

You twist the lure
caught in her lip, snip the barb,
and back it out of her mouth.

I hear their boots on the dock,
their coddling way with the girl,
whimpering now.

The Dead

I have cleaned out
the houses of death
too often to long for
possessions.

The dead have taken
if anything
too much care.
Their clocks never
run down,
their silverware
shines in its coats.

The dead have eaten
too much meat.
Some of us lie with them
still,

old letters
in frail hands.

Bluebeard's Wife

"Do not go into that room—"

For a long time she obeys.
Though it's hard to mistake
the scuttling in there,
the mission of flies,
a monstrous and mossy reek.

She's had so much practice
not-smelling the dead.

There's a maniac
throwing his body
over and over
against a trap door
in her mind.
There's an angel
behind the mirror.

I think she'll take her key
and hold it out like a wand.
I think she'll go down the stairs
in a trance of will.

And the murdered women
will stir
and try to remember their bodies
because of the light in her.

Sister Joanna Washes the Floor

Long after hours I slog
from scrubbing the bishop's kitchen.
A crack of light from the dining room

cuts the floor
and I dutifully check for bandits—
it's only himself, the rector,

the bishop's lawyer, and Father O'Toole.
Roman collars and ties loose,
Jack Daniel's making his rounds

though not to excess.
The cards catch my eye—
a deck worn soft

at the margins of mystery:
queens, kings, tricksters with all
the old glamour worn down to a blur

tamed and laid on the table.
I set down my slop bucket hard
and they jump. My suds

slosh on the tile. "It's Sister—"
the rector reminds them,
folding his hand.

He never remembers my name.
"You could slip on that floor,"
I say mildly. "I'll go for the mop."

It stands out under the moon.
Each frond frozen, the hair
of a virgin who's dead.

Above her the litter of stars,
a tarot of possibility
over my head.

Drifting

On the floor
of the South Bend, Indiana
Catholic Worker Shelter,
smelling home's bread,
I twitch from sleep,

rise to examine the street
like a superintendent of dark;
by habit, clutch for the keys
to houses long closed against me.
I jingle them
here in night's mouth.

Somewhere
deep in the rooms
an oven door slams
and all the bread in the world
is black with tears.

Flamenco Dancer

The man who played the guitar
has died or gone home
and when she goes to the edges
she goes alone.

Not even a line of music
under her feet,
a rhythm that breaks
as she heads for the margin of dance.

There on the brink of motion,
finding a gash in the wall,
art has to look for an exit—
now she has gone too far.

Becoming the space
love asks for:
the threshold,
the door.

*for Jean Donovan, a young
Maryknoll lay missionary, who
was murdered by government
soldiers, along with her three
nun-companions, in El Salvador,
December 2, 1980*

The Lost Child

Do not pity the lost child.
She has been lost so long,
she has become half wild.
She is afraid of nothing
so much as your care.
At night she sleeps in the rain,
wrapped in her hair.
She sings to herself
as brightly as any friend.
If you tame her, she will cry
and turn frail in the soft city.
Do not pity the lost child.
She has been lost so long,
she has become half wild.

L'Enfant sauvage

The men who came to see
the wild boy in his cage
had groomed themselves
as carefully as chimps.
They wore their wives
upon their arms
like guns.

For ten francs,
it was a disappointing show.
The wild boy stared,
slobbered, seeming to seek
eye teeth in the well-brushed muzzles,
nose twitching, seeming to scent
the milk-warm track
of wolf.

Monsieur l'abbaye Boudreau,
disciple of Port-Royal,
friend of Pascal,
was bitten on the thumb
and died of hydrophobia.

Miscarried

Unexpectedly
the rain
has ruined things.
We hurry to secure the tent,
and you remember
an image of Buddha:
clothes melting in rain,
everything sliding
into transparency.

I had a daughter
whose name also was Rain.
Sometimes I see her
in corners,
running
faster
than I.

Ritual

The one who knocked at the window
has flown away.

She who spoke once
on the threshold
is gone.

She has returned
to the nest of spirits.

She has refused
to enter the wind.

Once again we are sweeping
the stones of welcome,

setting a candle before the glass.

My Daughter Interrupts the Fairy Tale

With a strange cry . . .

No, not with the cry of the wild
swans, exactly,
but with the squawk of travelers
lost on the trail
blaming each other

With a strange cry, they flew out of the castle windows . . .

child, not as the wild swans lift,
as the sail fills,
as even the leaf-nosed bat
believes
Bernoulli's law—

but with the clumsy rush
of men resisting
an old enchantment

clearing the trees on an
angry and unsteady vector . . .

With a strange cry, they flew out of the castle windows
and over the park and the woods.

Persephone

I could still taste her milk
on my tongue as I entered
the village of hell.

She stayed home and beat
on the ground, she cried
for the grave to open—but I
loved terrible places, as girls will.

She overrated the droll affair:
I lolled in the dark, slept late,
ate from the fiend's lips
his single translucent seed.

But now, suns roll like pomegranates
up to the door and I skip for home.

No smell of garlic and bread
no garden, no bell.

I pick at the strings of her loom
crying—*where?*

Ashes blow on the hearth.
The child, Panic, clings to my hair.

As One Leaving

As one leaving a room
the last act to vacuum
right to the door.

Not a hair in the sink
nor a paring of nail
for an alien witch
to conjure my death.

As one leaving this way
I erase myself
from our tense
affection.

As one leaving a wound
I suture and clamp:
forgetting no vein to flood
no blood to remember
its way to the breath.

Separating the Eggs

Having seen too often
the woman's domestic motion:
yolk elided
from brown shell,
slick chorion
flicked
in a blue bowl

having seen too often
the angle of tawny braid,
tanned neck,
her red apron,
strong chords of her hands
too, tunneled with veins

having seen it, he dreams of oceans
beyond her window,
her tame hillock,
her island
of grass.

The Distaff

> . . . this would be the time for her to undo
> every knot on her garments, unlock the
> doors, open windows, uncork bottles, untie
> shoelaces, unbraid her hair, set the cows
> out of their stall, free the chickens, free
> anything that is tied.
>
> —Nor Hall, *The Moon and the Virgin*

The distaff drops
from our mother's fingers,
her voice, no longer
rising and falling
along the halls,
is still.

She lies in the grass,
her hair in a torn web,
the ribbons that laced her dress
drifting,
her shoelaces gone.

She cannot bear
the binding of silk,
patterns,
or spells.

She does not answer
to household words,
she is all
unwoven.

Abandoned Farmhouse

Why did they walk away,
leaving their house
alive as a dog
and desperate here on its own?

Maybe the Bank turned them out
and the panicky house had to hear them
pacing, pacing across its mind
till the key pinned a meaning in place
and left it there to go feral
the garden tendril by tendril slipping
into the woods.

Or maybe the man couldn't take
his wife's windows descrying,
refusing communion,
letting his soul's skin be the price
for dragging his boots through a room.
The fan of glass
over the door
shamed him, he had to head out.

The house has no will this winter
to cover her face from the wind.
So bent on collapsing
into the cellar,
resolving at last
her agony there:
the incomprehensible plumbing,
the foot on the stair.

The Gods Keep Descending

Just carrying in the groceries
you can lose everything.

Late October:
reeling
unreeling
intentional beat,
instinctive surrender—
the geese fly over.

"To be caught up like that!"
you allow—
stunned homesick
between the porch
and the car.

Your skin puckers, thins,
breaks into feathers

and easy as that we go,
belong to ourselves no longer
but to calling
and cliffs
of snow.

Icon

The deer have
hollowed
spaces
in the snow

they keep watch
under my window

I lie
in their
belly-shaped bowls

see
with their eyes,
as monks
learn to look
with an icon's gaze
at the monk
regarding the icon

see myself
out of a deer's stare
merely a blameless
grazer

veiled
in curious skin.

The Circus Dog

Every couple of days the train
pulls into some prairie town:
Northfield, Mankato, Cannon Falls.

Every couple of days the gymnasts sigh,
and the Flying Latvians mend their tights.
It's all to do over again.

The dog sees only the hoop of flame,
clowns dancing beyond.
He goes for it over and over.

Singed fur, eyelid melting into
perpetual droop. One more skid
to the sawdust in Couderay.

He's embarrassing to the troupe.
Nobody plays with him any more,
not even the ballerina on her trapeze

gets it. She looks away
from the dog-shaped hole
in the paper medallion,

his chilling obsession
with chance
his cockeyed religion

his furious
hunger
of will.

Variation on an Ancient Text

> If they ask my name, say that I lost it
> on the sea; if they ask my family, say
> that I am a shipwrecked man.
> —Apollonius of Tyre

I see the tide race
and my bones,
uncovered:
a rib cage
half buried in sand,
my face worn down
to its last mask.

What is the word
I will hear
in the sea's naming,
my ear become fossil,
unmade
in the stone's press?

Forgetting my art,
except to be shipwrecked
over and over.

Forgetting all language
but *Yes*
and again *Yes.*

Memory

I have been trees
and will be again
green cells
in the hearts of grass
or the snake's quick slide.
That I am swept
into a person
surprises the presences
sleeping in me,
who have been once
the hawk,
the rabbit,
and the glide.

Grotte du Grand Roc

(Périgord, Les Eyzies)

After eight months
the rain
finds my heart:
chrysanthemum
of stone
a mile below
what's real,

that bleat,
that candling green,
torment of hooves.

I miss the men
who painted here
as though to tell me
how to see,
painted the heart
of rock, of beast

        Know sacrifice
        Know purity
they said
        Surrender—

painted and went away.

The tongues
of rocks
extend by centuries.
I lick these drops
of rain—
        Know tears.

        Is someone calling me?
As if my heart
could swell

As if my heart
could open

If this rain
could melt
obsidian,
flood . . .

and I, the rock,
taste mercy
on my lips.

Clearing Land for the Lotus Pool

Wherever you lean
on a spade
in this earth of Duras
you strike the shells
of old houses

bones no one remembers
and, if you are quiet,
the spaces between
the bones.

"This land gives birth
to stones,"
my neighbor calls
as I pass
with the dogs.

He tosses the rocks
in a pile.
They roll together,
exchanging the names
of men and women,
stories of wounds,
a few notes of music
stones know.

These red tiles of Duras—
each holds
like a clay cup
the whisper we need
to sustain
our silence.

*Do what you've
listened to—*
says the cup
in my hands, smiling:

obey.

The Zen Master's Instructions

The meadow has become
a lake of rime:
another mirror.

In the dry stream bed
a white tail
flags its fear
some young one
unwilling to rest
with whatever rises
before the heart's eyes
as these other
watchers
have learned to do.

Stand like the deer
knowing the hunter
is in the woods
knowing her tremor
will bring the shot.

In your stillness
surrender
the hunter
over and over.

Sweeping the Zendo

Sweeping the zendo at dawn
a cramp of concentration,
then the light:
I do not wish to transcend
suffering and grief.

Were you to slide
like smoke, Grief,
into form, here
on these flagstones,
a starving ghost,
I would weep
at your knees
crying *Mother!*
Dear Life!

Were you to strut
this floor, Suffering,
sleek pheasant in plume,
I would steal feathers
to hang
in my hair.

Home Farm

After some time
blackberry vines gather
around your table.

The roof tree
does not remember you,
falls, finally,
old nailing undone,
into the tumble
of thorn.

You stood so long
at that window
hearing the tap of vines:
relentless desire—

green nails that dug
like your own,
longing that pulled you
from bed before dawn
down to the lambing pens,
longing that dragged
the plow

Desire drove your hands
in the dough,
flicked from
each moment
a clear bubble
and sent it
floating
over the grass.

The beam still stands
over your bed.
I think the stones
hold also
love cries,
birth cries,

here where you cradled
the winter lamb,
sucked out its death
with your own mouth;
where two of you
held the lamb
in your bed's heat
till it chose, stretched,
and entered its life—

that inviolate day
nothing not done for loving
floats
over the choke
of vines.

Before Spring

Feathering out his red shawls
the cardinal attends to
groundfeeding, his green mate's
whistle, becoming
a minor flamenco
low on the osier dogwood,
brittle with March.

Purled together,
you and I fall asleep,
surrender our bodies like angels
reversing gears.

Lao T'zu tells of a kind of knowing
that tints the soul,
surviving birth after birth,
as if soul wore a bolt of crimson,
flying and pinned,

as if love could stream on and on
like a flag on the wind.

Snowblind

Driving backroads to Northfield
in drifting snow,
losing the lay of farms
and the lift of sky,
I'm forced to enter the prairie.
Sun's glare
erases the margin.
It's all white to you then—
a rapture like divers feel
leaving air, memory of land:
love's hands, the gray cup
of a junco.
Surrendered to longing,
a flare opens under the bone,
a wound you pour from
into the prairie light.

We Keep Asking the Prairie

I'm drawn into the clearing,
a remnant prairie skirted in oaks
now in their brown season.

A doe stalls in the woods,
shook by her longing to break
into plain space:

this is a well she could fall down forever
loose enough to be scattered,
her myths untwining in streamers of DNA.

Hawks circle,
abandoned to updraft,
river birch gather to practice jumps.

As if we all come here to fall
and take off again,
tumblers in love.

Durham

for Robin Fox

This might be considered
a waste of time: to sit
still at a window, telling
one bud from another.

How does he see his life—
the oriole
bayed in quince blossom,
flounce big as his head?
He at least lights,
starts a beak into each bowl.
The hummingbird
keeps her motor running.
Her own purr of desire
blowing, I guess,
some process in pollen
head over tail.
The yellow warbler
tumbles down branches of lilac
hitting at each rest
the skin of dreams
he will seek until death.

Where did it go? they will ponder:
the day's profligate grace
how they flew,
flummoxed among choices,
their busy fall—

while we were hung
like tongues
in the bell
of our whole desire.

When I Imagine My Soul

When I imagine my soul
I think of a bear,
shambling across tundra.
I think she's escaped from a circus,
the scars of a ring in her nose:
fat, loping, patient, untiring bear.

Her paws slap and click
bound for the edge of Alaska.
She will plunge at last
into constellations of ice,
swimming without ideas.

Even there
I imagine her torn muzzle
bent north,
feel in my nerves
her relentless
continual
swim.

Bees in Autumn

It has rained for three days.
They all dream of dissolution.
Few make it back at night.
They have surrendered themselves
to dying flowers.

At this season, the bees seem old,
solving as though on thick limbs
the problem of chicory. To one,
sunflower becomes the face of a clock.
He must dangle himself from each hour
hung by a dried-up will,
blame God for abandoning him.
I am busy, busy, he hums
out of habit. He hates her
for not letting go the sweetness
his legs want to haul
once more to the hive.

Why?

croons the other,
sunk in love's body.
He longs only to swoon,
deep in September,
the sun on his gold fur.

The dead stand, laughing,
before the hive.
This, too, dissolves,
they are singing,
*this habit of skin. An opinion
controlled by the intricate motion
of hair on a bee's thigh.*

The busy one listens,
always ready to die.

The one up to his hips in love
will fall asleep in the snow,
wake up still kissing his flower.
The dead have gone laughing by.

Hasidic Bride

You will lie
above me
the length of the bridal
sheet

cry about Canaan
into my hair
and sleep all night
with your hand
on my thigh—

tell me
how lovers can fly
to the caves of mercy—
breathe with my breath.

Because I have sworn
to remember
your benediction of flesh.

Portrait of Madame Monet on Her Deathbed

All the while she was dying, I could not stop painting her face.
—Monet, writing in his journal at Vétheuil

He will paint her again as grain;
now she is fog
the chantilly fog of the Seine:

avoiding no hint of the slow dissolve,
the bandage around her jaw,
rigor's cramp at the lip,
how death abraded and hollowed her,
while he remembered light.

Had he a failed heart
or a wholly transfigured eye
that knew her tonight as water
convulsion and sky?
that stared through layers of the body
at more than it took to die?

Passover

Art is what remains when the pot is broken.

—Chinese proverb

I know we are bound to the earth,
and the cracked heart, old terra cotta,
surrenders to vine.

              Listen—I've seen
wind stir the hair of the dead at Belsen,
growing like art from the lacing grass;

what is terrible, even, rises.
The ruined pot dreams of ignition,
each molecule coddles its flame.

Enough alphabet for a torah
sits on the tongue. And all shards
from the winds' end gather again.

I know we are bound to the earth
by desire's green thread
or the milk snake's slippery pass.

Hepatica splits now from its leaf-wing.
Out of the vessel's wreck,
inwardness forms on the air

and that ghost tenderly enters
the soul of some mortal thing.

Boreal Owl

"How is the dark for you?"
she's demanding,
stark on a red oak
over the snow,

archaic face bent
to the job, wearing
a listening look
that obligates even her prey,

safe, now, in their tunnels
under the crust, too new
to conceive of grace:
still

they acknowledge her shadow,
its image
out of the darkness
behind the ears.

When I close my eyes
she is standing,
feathered in sun,
holding the hunt

on a nerve's edge.
Longing, she says,
compels nothing.
Not even a mouse to run.

Tundra Swan

Silence pulls her
along the rim of all that she knows.

Into the eyes of a dark lake—
which needs, too, the impetus
of her gaze to arouse—
she stares and descends.

Black paddles wag, rudder
her awkward plunge.

And when we come back
she's asleep

as though the perilous trip
all went
for a sculpted dream
in a white sphere

as though this passage
(she tells me)
heads back to the dark drum:

incandescence and night
a vision for sealed eyes
whatever we looked at then.

Field Guide to North Shore Geology

The stones are telling each other lies
about gems hid in their cracked hearts,
bragging about hot times in the magma
when they were molten and ran around.
They are all in love with a flashy rock
in the sky. Souls preen at the quartz
windows, trying to catch her eye.

North Coast

> The moment when the soul parts on itself
> in desire is conceived of as a dilemma of
> body and senses.
>
> —Anne Carson, *Eros the Bittersweet*

Here on the rim of the inland sea
lights flicker and lie.
Everything technical falters,
everything mortal dies.

Now and then, on a mission,
gull-wise, a soul flies:
white feathers against the dark,
breaking,
and breaking spray.

It feels like a rip in fabric
left so long in the attic
it has to give;
fibers grown soft in their long rest,
red faded to gray.

Soul lifts
from its rifted mammal,
looks at its fellow souls,
each hoping to enter some granite thing
or a stolid wave;
only the play here of lightning flung
on the water's face.

Wind rising;
moths flutter against the pane,
nerves tell them it's twilight.

As if the dead were valuable,
waves bear them along,
flesh into luminous tendrils
bones into bedrock,
porphyry,
common ground.

It Began

It began, then, the war that never ended,
though for a while we kept doing the old things:
shopping thrift stores, digging through bins of toys,
looking for plain clothing a little worn.

Winter, in that latitude, never forgave;
but we could pay off the electric,
buy pills for the dog when she got sick.
There was mulled wine left over from Christmas
and two bags of candles somebody found on sale.

We kept putting suet out for the birds,
drowsed in the south window as we had always done,
watching the purple finches,
getting the last of the game.

We saw light mauled in the alders,
the traveling shadow claim our yard,
our street becoming the crust
over a bowl of flame.

The Crossing

All night we were moving, stopped often but not long:
searchlight, screech of brake on the siding,
sometimes the rose of a man's hand, lit from within
as he tended a pipe or grabbed a smoke between jobs,
flares of border language in polyglot tongues.
Dawn's finger tapped at a slit in the board—
you cried out in your sleep.

Sometimes I don't know whether I'm dreaming my dreams
or yours, or just leaning back quiescent in
somebody's brain. It's only when I feel calm or glad
or even afraid that I know I'm asleep.
Only when I feel anything.
Maybe that woman leaning against the glass
of her office window is dreaming us as we pass.
Or that man at the turnstile, his spectacles catching a flame—
he puts a crease in the *Times,*
folds it under his arm,
turns down the brim of his hat
in the precious rain.

Open All Night

You call from a motel off the Interstate, somewhere near Coeur d'Alene,
once a confection, wallpaper pink and flocked with floral bouquets.
It holds a musk of cigarettes, Shalimar, This-Bud's-For-You:
some rooms hang on to things that were good at the time.

You call from a place you thought you had left;
you'd showered, put on a fresh shirt, gotten your cleanliness back
on the road, forgetting or being too young to know
the room has you forever.

Your fingers trace velvety paper, bald at the seam;
so many men make this motion, trying to get a line out.
The air conditioner spits out the cold air America cans,
the mattress, covered in plastic, pushes away.

Driving West

Books lean
from their shelves
like children wanting to get in the car,

luggage opens its mouth,
gaping, while I decide.
Meanwhile,

the soul hides, smiling.
She loves to travel. She has her own plans.
She hopes I wake up in a ditch near Provo,

get amnesia, walk into a cow town
without a stitch of skin on the ego;
she wants to graze on a new kind of grass.

The soul doesn't care
where I put the Triple-A maps
or the cell phone.

The soul hopes
I run out of gas.
Plan on finding the thing you need

in the dumpster, don't plan at all;
it comes to the same thing.
Obsess over maps, tide charts, coastal markers:

you go under anyway, weighed down by a backpack
heavy with gathered stones. If the waves need you,
they'll sweep up the coast.

At my feet, a shelf of fossil clams,
all through these rocks the smile or winged gesture,
detritus of ancient life. A bank of mollusks preserved

in an image of interdependence they didn't mean,
a cozy city feeding and sleeping,
caught by some fiery purpose sweeping it into form.

Green Herons

For a while I saw green herons everywhere
after I got the knack of picking them out
of the hemlock and wetland grass.
I knew them up close
with their unkempt head feathers
just out of bed,
the crazy look of concentration
before they stab for the eyes.
Then all at once they disappeared
or I lost the bond, the latter of course,
as newborns—you know from their gaze—
remember God or *something* punk-headed
and focused, and slightly deranged.

Scholar's Garden

for Parker Palmer

Crows fly over the scholar's garden.
He wants them to be ravens,
longs to see the thick beak and intelligent eye,
a bird poised for conversation
who will admire with him
an old calligraphy in its frame of space.

The scholar sips tea, tries his teeth on a nut shell.
He once knew a raven who spoke Mandarin passably well,
who tried to teach him the words of a far, dark people
across the sea.
That raven would sit everyday over the moongate,
contrasting the scholar's measured wisdom
with some frantic, ardent,
evolving theology.

Just as the old man began to feel
the strenuous energy of conversion
coursing along the meridians
even down to the blue veins
under the nail,
the raven rustled and flew
as though he had gotten a letter.

Now the scholar sits on his silk pillow,
no hope to recover tranquility
due his years, his honors,
watching the sky.

Infinite Day

Shining confetti of beach plastic at the tideline,
      weathered green, orange, the azure everyone loves,
            hues that draw housewives to buy bleach bottles, washing detergent,

all the yellows that make work smile back at the worker,
      plastic of children's toys, guaranteed to raise the IQ,
            boatly gew-gaws and oil containers to make motors hum.

Gather the white sterile dreams of a death-denying city,
      crushed random among prayers:
            I sing of shredded tampon dispensers whorled into scrimshaw,

syringes with infinite calibration. I prance in the ruin of all stuff,
      want to reclaim, recycle, redeem and return, paste
            all of this rosy glister onto an icon of Christ Pantocrator,

or Michael the Archangel, give it all wings again.
      Nothing is wasted. All the four doors of the universe
            shut and whale back every bright bauble; America's shore

plays with its plastic curlers over and over,
      transfigures the body and blood. Lovers! Made of star matter
            out of an intergalactic diamond mine!

You have ground yourselves into Bakelite and Pyrex,
      learned to refract at last
            the unbearable shine.

Seascape

The practical lace of the oyster's gill
out on her banks
takes it and leaves it. Egret,
poised on a scaffold of yellow legs, says nothing.
What you hear
is the lisp of your own longing,
whirled in the ear.

The oyster knows
how to inhabit her iridescence,
allows just a photon of light
to take her back to the prom.
Her shell is so full of glitter,
how could she work
without restraining the sun's intent?

Loss is the channel, she tells me,
through which we enter the world.

Speaking in Tongues

I go to church every Sunday
though I don't believe a word of it,
because the longing for God
is a prayer said in the bones.

When people call on Jesus
I move to a place in the body
where such words rise,
one of the valleys
where hope pins itself to desire;
we have so much landscape like that
you'd think we were made
to sustain a cry.

When the old men around me
lift their hands
as though someone has cornered them,
giving it all away,
I remember a dock on the estuary,
watching a heron get airborne against the odds.
It's the transitional moment that baffles me—
how she composes her rickety
grocery cart of a body
to make that flight.

The pine siskin, stalled on a windy coast,
remembers the woods
she will long for when needs arise; so
the boreal forest composes itself in my mind:
first as a rift, absence,
then in a tumble of words
undone from sense, like a stutter
you hear when somebody falls
over the cliff of language. Call it a gift.

The Deer's Prayer

Sometimes I'm bigger
than my body;
I can't help it.

Dawn stirs me this way
scent of fir tree and moss
rivulets under the hoof.

Released from fear,
sometimes I slide into grace.
Having run far and fast

to preserve my hide,
I lie and let it all leave me,
the facts I tried to protect.

I feel the earth turn
like a fawn in the belly
and lose the knack of telling

what I inhabit
from what inhabits me.

Two Biker Chicks

(after Andrew Marvell)

The body likes it here
and wants the soul
to vacation at least
on the Oregon coast.

These two get along
like old biker chicks
who don't make love anymore
but still fight over the road maps
zip their bags together at night.

I'll tell you whose side I'm on
in this ruckus,
watching the green rain
slide down the glass:

the one who makes dinner
and stands with binoculars at the door,
waiting for herons,
the one whose big dog
is slapping his tail on the floor.

It's Not Safe at All

Weather spilled all night on the house.
The radio, often erratic, delivered an alto voice
to my bedroom at 2:00 a.m. I got up, made tea for the visitor,
somewhere in Devon, telling the world news.

Coyote, burned white in the lights of the motion detector,
loped into the woods.

A yellow plastic Safeway bag,
sodden with all the night's fuss,
wheels down the hill. I wake to hail
on the skylight, the drag of consciousness
out of the quilt.

Nothing happens for day after day of our lives;
what comes to pass stands out like calligraphy
on the empty space, precious as real estate.

Snow, now, fills in the mountain behind a spruce,
always a few branches waiting to preen
before the wind gets them, make a statement
just as the background melts away.

Over and over again like this,
something risks speaking,
snatches the chance to be known,
as each of us climbed on a molecule,
once, rode it down like a pickup
into the chimneys, the town.

I think of a deer lying down to sleep in her hollow:
all other species ride out of her dream.
First the dream hovers, fragile as luna moth,
transparent sea jelly,
gains substance until they all fall over the edge,
delicate toes and webbing, hoof and wing,
splitting out of their eggs and amnions,
scaly and smiling,
damp with the fluid of deer's dreams.

Call It a Match

From the hermit crab I could learn to own nothing.
Deer pick their way without mortgages up the slope,
Stellar's Jay cranks out his expectation of bread.

What am I trading for salary?
Christmas of all the world's dumpsters
sifts into the Goodwill store.
I think of my father, that natty man,
laid out in his paper dress.

There's a light in the bone bleached by my door.
What body the bone belonged to I cannot tell,
what fears drove it, what grief,
how it flared out in its manner of loving,
what species of young it dropped in the wet grass.

Call it love anyway, call it a match,
green bone to spruce, feather/ephemeral leaf.

Autobiography

You can hear corn grow in my life,
it's the only whisper in town, except what that girl
in her cotton gown confides to her husband,
just as he kills the light.

Go and find the gray ocean pawing her sand:
What have you brought me? she cries. *Skeins of mist*
from the high country, dry as used breath.
I swim out with a load of warm souls,

women who want to be sea lions,
children who pulled back before birth.
How they will love each other,
away from the skin of the earth.

The Visit

Things don't work well in this house.
It must have burned out, she says,
sitting in darkness. Only one burner

lights on the stove, the rest
crusted with grease.
Bags of newspapers block the front door.

She says she goes out every day,
afraid you'll put her away
on a clean shelf, as she put

her mother. What we fear
are the things we ourselves have done
and believe it is right to do.

What we love are the words
mothers say in books, tragic mothers
who die young, leaving a child

in the snow. We know she will send
an angel, light a miraculous fire,
hold us in sleep—even now

I feel her hand on my forehead,
lean to the lull of her voice.

The Lives of the Cousins

The lives of the cousins came in letters
from our Canadian aunts,
with graduation photos from nursing school:

O pure cousins in navy capes
gold pin at the neck,
organdy cupcake upended on practical hair.

Carmen and I skidded, crazy as boys,
through the tiled hall, we were striped
with the welts we toweled on each other,

making the puppies yap. How could we,
dripping and screaming,
dream of becoming Cousins?

Quiet and kind and black and white on the wall
the nurses, unjudging anything, sat.
I could not think of my brown hands

holding each other, smelling of Jergens,
on such a white lap. I could not think of my
pink nails unbitten, toes curled in rubber-soled shoes

walking my heart down a hospital corridor
after a cart. The cousins dimmed
in the lamplight, flanked on each side

by Jesus and Mary, their hearts
fileted on their chests, each squeezed
by its bracelet of thorns.

The Foster Child

Weaving a basket of the day, they
who seldom spoke otherwise
talked in bed.

It was not a house for privacy:
two rooms and a sleeping porch;
I on my couch overheard
everything said.

Propped on pillows, he smoked a pipe,
she fingered rosary beads,
between them the basket was finished

and put aside in the methodical way
they did everything:
played cribbage, carted the leaves away.

No ideas hung on the blackberry vine
they wove into the warp of real things,
words for *mice, feathers,* and *wings,*

for the white cat who loved them,
birch trees and wrens.
A few feet from the door

the waves kept lapping.
I'd never been given before
a sense of containment,

and never got it again,
except I can weave it now on my own,
out of the talk and stillness of that home.

Shin Ohashe Bridge

In Hiroshige's print of Shin Ohashe Bridge,
people are coming and going over a frail span.
Black crosshatching etches a sudden shower.
The travelers raise parasols,
pruned to bare feet, white schoolgirl stockings.
Surrendered to their geometry,
two men cringe under an oiled triangle.

The ephemeral bridge goes nowhere
and none of these people,
for all of their hurry, will get home.
Under the delicate girders,
water begins its ascent to the sky.

The people are trying so hard to cross,
not knowing how deeply etched
are the lines of rain
that hold them in place;
how implacable that rain,
which seems just an afternoon trial
between temple and teahouse.
They do not know what black scratches
pin them forever to his page.